JEFF BURTON

Jeff Burton

Dale Earnhardt Jr.

Famous Finishes

Famous Tracks

Kenny Irwin Jr.

Jimmie Johnson

The Labonte Brothers

Lowriders

Monster Trucks & Tractors

Motorcycles

Off-Road Racing

Rockcrawling

Tony Stewart

The Unsers

Rusty Wallace

JEFF BURTON

June Ford

with additional text by **Jeff Gluck**

CHELSEA HOUSE
P U B L I S H E R S

A Haights Cross Communications Company ®

Philadelphia

Cover Photo: Veteran driver Jeff Burton finished the 2004 season on a high note after getting a fresh start with the Richard Childress team.

CHELSEA HOUSE PUBLISHERS

VP, NEW PRODUCT DEVELOPMENT   Sally Cheney
DIRECTOR OF PRODUCTION   Kim Shinners
CREATIVE MANAGER   Takeshi Takahashi
MANUFACTURING MANAGER   Diann Grasse

STAFF FOR JEFF BURTON

EDITORIAL ASSISTANT Sarah Sharpless
PRODUCTION EDITOR Bonnie Cohen
PHOTO EDITOR Pat Holl
SERIES DESIGN AND LAYOUT Hierophant Publishing Services/EON PreMedia

Original edition first published in 2001.

http://www.chelseahouse.com

A Haights Cross Communications ✦ Company ®

First Printing

1   3   5   7   9   8   6   4   2

Library of Congress Cataloging-in-Publication Data

Ford, June, 1957–
    Jeff Burton/June Ford with additional text by Jeff Gluck.
        p. cm.—(Race car legends. Collector's edition)
    Includes bibliographical references and index.
    ISBN 0-7910-8699-2
    1. Burton, Jeff, 1967—Juvenile literature. 2. Automobile racing drivers—United
States—Biography—Juvenile literature. I. Gluck, Jeff, 1980– II. Title. III. Series.
GV1032. B87F67 2005
796.72'092—dc22

                                                                    2005010393

TABLE OF CONTENTS

1

A NEW START

The hurtful talk picked up in 2004. Critics said Jeff Burton, one of NASCAR's good guys, was near the end of his career. He can't win anymore, they said. He's washed up, they said.

Even Jack Roush, who had loyally owned the car Jeff drove for most of the driver's career, agreed to release him from his job. But Jeff Burton wasn't about to quit.

Another car owner, Richard Childress, signed Jeff to drive for him. Jeff never let himself get down and finished 2004 on a high note.

"I think it's important to never quit," Jeff told the media. "When things aren't going well you . . . have several choices. One of them is to just give up; the other one is just to keep fighting. That's what I've chosen to do not only with the year, but with my career."[1]

Jeff Burton was 37 years old in 2004, much older than the "Young Guns," the drivers who were in their twenties. But after spending so long with Roush, Jeff said he cherished a new chance and a fresh start.

"The thing that stuck out at me, that really jumped at me right off the bat is [Childress is] a friendly place to be," he said. "You know, people aren't at each other's throats. We have problems, but we're all trying to fix 'em."[2]

Once Jeff got into his new car with the Richard Childress team, he recorded 11 top-15 finishes out of the final 14 races of 2004.

Jeff didn't have too many problems as 2004 came to a close. Once he got into his new car, driving for Richard Childress's team, Jeff recorded 11 top-15 finishes out of the final 14 races, including three top-10s and a top-five.

A new team could mean more success for Jeff. In July 2003, *Associated Press* said Jeff "has been something of an invisible man the last few seasons." That comment was made because Jeff had finished in the top five of the Nextel Cup standings (formerly called the Winston Cup) in four consecutive years. But, in 2003, Jeff hadn't won a race since 2001, so the pressure was building and the critics were talking.

"When you're running well, your competitors come and talk to you because they're fishing for information," Jeff told

Jeff Burton waits while the crew works on his car during practice at Lowe's Motor Speedway in May of 2004. He had not won a race since 2001, and critics were talking.

the *Associated Press* in March 2003. "When you're not running well, you can feel the distance grow. I don't like that. I like to be in the middle of things."[3]

Roush expressed confidence in Jeff at the time, saying, "It's just a matter of time until he is back in Victory Circle."[4]

But that support wasn't backed by a sponsor. With his position at Roush suddenly unstable, Jeff left the team for Childress. Jeff said he couldn't wait to prove his critics wrong.

"When I accepted the position to drive this car, I did it knowing that Richard [Childress] wanted me to come in and

New teammate Kevin Harvick, right, jokes with Jeff Burton during a news conference at the Bristol Motor Speedway in Bristol, Tennessee, on April 2, 2005.

be a leader and more than just a guy who shows up on Friday afternoon to sit in the car," he told *USA Today* in early 2005. "I relish that opportunity."[5]

Jeff was immediately welcomed to his new team. Kevin Harvick was a member of NASCAR's "Young Guns" group, but Jeff was regarded as the team's veteran driver. Childress said bringing Jeff on board would give the team a more mature, experienced leader. It would also take pressure off Harvick.

"(Jeff) knows the cars, he knows the chassis, he knows a lot about what it takes to be consistent and win," Childress said. "I think it's going to be a huge plus for us."[6]

For his part, Jeff relished the chance to start over. Even though he was 37 years old, he said he felt much younger.

DID YOU KNOW?

The trend in NASCAR racing is for drivers to be young. That means veterans like Jeff Burton are becoming rare.

After the 2003 season, former Nextel Cup champion Bill Elliott retired. Then, two-time Nextel Cup winner Terry Labonte called it quits in 2004. Legends Mark Martin and Rusty Wallace are scheduled to step down after the 2005 season.

Meanwhile, drivers in their early twenties have become common. In early 2005, rookie Kyle Busch made his full-time Nextel Cup debut at the tender age of 19.

Jeff's brother, Ward, couldn't find a job at the beginning of the 2005 season.

"[Ward is] a capable driver," Jeff told *USA Today*. "Unfortunately, he's gotten caught up in the fact that people want to hire 12-year-olds."*

*USA Today/January 20, 2005/Page 11C.

"I've been around a long time, but I'm only 37," he said. "I'll tell you right now, if I was as good a driver at 30 or 32 as I am now, I'd have won a lot more races. I can honestly tell you I'm better today than I was five years ago."[7]

Whether his ability will translate into newfound success remains to be seen in 2005.

② A GO-KART FAMILY

Jeff Burton was born on June 29, 1967, into what he describes as an average American family. Living in the rural, blue-collar town of South Boston, Virginia, his parents, John and Meredith Burton, already had two boys—six-year-old Ward and three-year-old Brian—when their third son entered the world.

One day Jeff's dad, who owned a construction company, brought home a two-seater go-kart for the three brothers. Two weeks later, eight-year-old Ward was competing at the small local go-kart track. At home, it was common to see Ward driving his two brothers around the yard, maneuvering around obstacles, as Jeff, then a toddler, bounced around in the side seat.

By the time Jeff was five, he was watching Ward and their father build go-karts. He was still so small that he stood on his tiptoes to watch them race. Eventually, all three brothers and their father were building and racing go-karts.

"When I became old enough to race, Dad quit racing because he couldn't drive and work on all the karts. I was seven at the time, and having me work on the go-karts would do more harm than good," Jeff told *NASCAR Winston Cup Illustrated*.

All three Burton brothers and their father built and raced go-karts. Jeff began racing at age seven.

Unbeknownst to John Burton, that first go-kart he'd brought home for his boys had set in motion a course that would one day take two of his sons into the elite world of the NASCAR Nextel Cup Series. But for now, go-karting had become the family's hobby. "I ran go-karts for nine years and progressed up through the ranks. Brian won more state championships than any of the rest of us did," Jeff recalled.

Twice, Jeff won the Virginia State Go-kart Championship, but being a professional stock car driver was just a pipe dream.

Besides, the Burton boys weren't just interested in go-karts. They were active in school sporting events, hunting, and fishing, and they enjoyed their friends, who always seemed to be meeting at the Burtons' house, especially on Sundays—race day—to watch the races on TV.

By the time he was 15, the family's go-kart hobby had kindled Jeff's interest in racing late-model stock cars.

Sometimes, John Burton would take his boys to the races at Darlington Raceway in South Carolina, as well as to North Carolina Speedway in Rockingham. They'd travel in a small motor home, camp out, and go to the Sunday race. At the time, Jeff idolized Cale Yarborough, who, from his first win in 1965 until he retired in 1988, won three NASCAR Cup championships and had 83 career victories.

When he wasn't racing, Jeff attended Halifax County High School. He was an outstanding athlete, playing basketball and soccer and also serving as captain of the soccer team.

At 15, Jeff's interest gradually moved from go-karts to late-model stock cars on short tracks. He had begun helping a racer in his hometown work on a late-model car. When Jeff

While there are many go-kart tracks all over the United States, the best place to go-kart for fun is at a NASCAR SpeedPark.

NASCAR SpeedParks feature up to eight tracks with go-karts of all shapes, speeds, and sizes.

Rookies and veterans have plenty of chances to race. Each track has a sign that tells drivers who is best suited to race on that track.

One track even features half-sized Nextel Cup cars, although a driver's license is required to drive one of those.

Unfortunately, only five NASCAR SpeedParks exist: Myrtle Beach, South Carolina; Concord, North Carolina; Seiverville, Tennessee; St. Louis, Missouri; and Toronto, Canada.

wasn't racing go-karts, he would go with the racer and help work on his race car.

One day after one of the races, a driver went to Victory Lane and punched out the winner. The driver was suspended for three races. Desperate for a driver for their Pure Stock entry, the suspended driver's team asked Jeff to drive. To just about everyone's surprise, Jeff won the race. A career was born.

3

SIBLING REV-ALRY

Jeff's surprise win wasn't without complications. He and his oldest brother, Ward, were competing in the same field. While the two young men shared a passion for cars, they were separated by many differences. With a six-year age span between them, they were not raised in the same way, and the opportunities they received to develop their driving skills were not the same either. They had different interests, and sometimes the competition between the two brothers became personal.

Ward was influenced by their grandfather's interests in wildlife, fishing, and hunting. Jeff was influenced more by their father's interest in sports. Jeff followed college basketball and is a devoted fan of the Duke Blue Devils men's basketball team. Jeff is patient. Ward is more aggressive. Jeff prefers living in a neighborhood. Ward prefers the country life. For reasons neither of them understands, they even speak with different accents.

Early on, Jeff focused on racing and convinced his parents to invest his freshman college savings fund in cars. Soon, the sophomore funds were invested as well. In contrast, Ward had started at the bottom of the local racing scene, driving a Volkswagen. He was lucky to have a good set of tires for each

Jeff (left) shares a passion for racing with his brother Ward. The two once fought after wrecking both their cars in a race, but the brothers now learn from each other both on and off the track.

race and rarely had new tires. Jeff, on the other hand, had new tires every racing weekend. Ward later admitted that at first he'd been jealous of his youngest brother's advantages.

The brothers' introduction to street- and late-model stock car racing was far from illustrious. Both often worked all night in dingy, damp little buildings on cars. It didn't look like there was much of a future in racing, and their brother Brian had already abandoned racing for college. Jeff, who was having a tough time, recalled later that at that point he didn't think he'd ever make it on the circuit.

In 1986, at age 19, Jeff became the youngest driver in NASCAR history to win a late-model stock car race.

"I don't race because it's fun to race. I race because it's fun to beat other people at the game, whatever that game is," Jeff said. And sometimes that competitor was his brother. This left the Burton family with a problem: how to celebrate winning with one brother while comforting the other brother over his loss.

Although the two men are now supportive of each other, that was not always the case. Once in 1987, they were both racing late-model stock cars in a hometown competition. Their whole family had come to watch. With only a few laps remaining in the race, Ward was near the top of the track trying to pass a car for the lead when Jeff, who was below him, pulled under Ward. They both wrecked. Angry, Ward came down the track after Jeff.

"I got out of my car and went over to his car, and I had him by the neck, squeezing it. I happened to look up and I saw Daddy coming. I decided right then it was a real good time for me to get my butt to the hauler and get out of sight," Ward recalled.

"It got ugly," Jeff explained. "We got into a shoving match in front of everyone and embarrassed our entire family, and the worst part was our mom was disappointed with us." He added, "We never, at least since we have matured as adults, have done that to each other again." Their relationship improved afterward, and they again began to learn from each other, on and off the track.

"Ward has always taken care of me. He always looked out for me," Jeff told *NASCAR Winston Cup Illustrated*. Ward had learned the importance of sponsors and the business side of racing. He helped Jeff establish himself as a driver.

On the track, they were no longer brother against brother, but competitors aiming for Victory Lane. Each admits he likes to see the other win but not at his own expense. And each says the other is his favorite driver.

Ward Burton helped his brother Jeff in his early racing days, advising him on the business side of the sport.

Jeff won five more late-model stock division events and became the Orange County Speedway co-champion in 1987. He won seven events and was voted most popular driver at South Boston Speedway the following year. By 1989, Jeff was ready to move into the NASCAR Busch Series, Grand National Division.

Only the most elite drivers move into the NASCAR divisions. To be successful, drivers need more than skill, persistence, competitive spirit, and tenacity. They need a great car, a good pit crew, and lots of money.

For that money, they look for sponsors: a company, team, or individual to help offset the cost of cars, parts, fees, crashes, crews, salaries, travel, and other necessary expenses. It is difficult for up-and-coming drivers to find sponsors or even car owners to take them on. "The Busch Series teaches you how to handle things," Jeff told the *Virginian-Pilot*. "When I raced Late Models at South Boston, I knew I was going to finish in the top five every week. But when I went to Busch, I didn't know if I was going to make the race."

Jeff worked and drove hard. In 1988, driving for his father, Jeff competed in five Busch Grand National races: three in a Chevrolet and two in an Oldsmobile. He didn't even place within the top 10. He ended the season 44th in points standings. By 1989, still driving for his dad, but this time in a Pontiac, he decided to make a run at the NASCAR Busch Series Rookie of the Year award. Although he didn't make it, he finished the season with 27 starts, 2 top-5s, and 6 top-10s. He was 13th in the standings.

Jeff changed to a Buick for his 1990 season and drove for series legend Sam Ard. He won his first Busch Series race in Martinsville, Virginia. In the fall race at Michigan Speedway, he took his first Busch Series pole. To win the pole, a racer must have the highest qualifying speed. At the race, the pole winner is the first car in the lineup, or grid. It's the position everyone wants. Jeff finished the year at 15th in the standings.

The following year, he drove for Bill Papke in a variety of models and won in his hometown. He finished the year 12th in the standings and had 31 starts, 1 win, 3 top-5s, 10 top-10s, and 2 poles.

In December 1992, Jeff married his junior high school sweetheart, Kim Browne. Kim tried to travel with him as often as possible and could usually be found by his side throughout the circuit. Jeff also had his best season to date in the Busch Series. He was driving for FILMAR Motorsports and drove Oldsmobiles, with the exception of one race at Dover International Speedway, where he drove a Ford. He won at the New Hampshire International Speedway (NHIS) in Loudon, New Hampshire. He had 31 starts, 1 win, 4 top-5s, 10 top-10s, and finished the year 9th in the standings.

But 1993 proved to be a turning point in Jeff's career. He drove for several owners and won in Myrtle Beach, South Carolina, with Ward coming in second. Jeff drove a Ford and finished the Busch year with 28 starts, 1 win, 3 top-5s, 10 top-10s, and he placed 14th in the rankings.

The Busch Series is often called the "junior" series because the drivers who excel in it "graduate" to the most prestigious races, the Nextel Cup Series.

Jeff made his NASCAR Nextel Cup debut in 1993 in the inaugural race at Loudon, in which he qualified sixth. It was his only NASCAR Nextel Cup race of the season, but he caught the eye of the Stavola brothers (Billy and Mickey Stavola), who signed him to their team. Although Jeff would be expected to work publicity spots, he would have regular sponsors. Jeff wouldn't have to spend as much time raising money, so he would have more time to concentrate on driving.

"I wasn't thinking about [Nextel] Cup racing, I had all the car owner I could stand, and he'd had all of me he could stand, and my option was [Nextel] Cup racing, and that's why I went Cup racing," Jeff told the *Richmond Times-Dispatch*. "I thought the Busch Series was perfect for me,

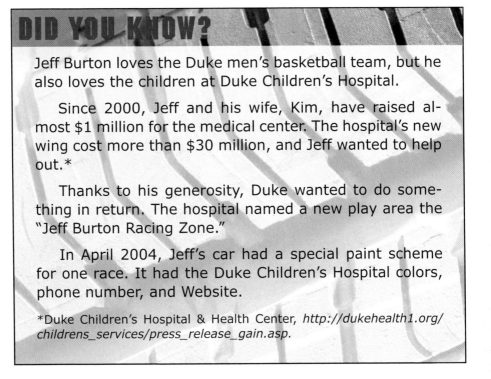

DID YOU KNOW?

Jeff Burton loves the Duke men's basketball team, but he also loves the children at Duke Children's Hospital.

Since 2000, Jeff and his wife, Kim, have raised almost $1 million for the medical center. The hospital's new wing cost more than $30 million, and Jeff wanted to help out.*

Thanks to his generosity, Duke wanted to do something in return. The hospital named a new play area the "Jeff Burton Racing Zone."

In April 2004, Jeff's car had a special paint scheme for one race. It had the Duke Children's Hospital colors, phone number, and Website.

*Duke Children's Hospital & Health Center, *http://dukehealth1.org/ childrens_services/press_release_gain.asp.*

and I enjoyed it and loved it and never really gave much thought to [Nextel] Cup until I got into it."

Jeff wasn't the only one in his family headed for the Cup Series. Ward was going there, too.

4

ROOKIE OF THE YEAR

Despite the fact that Jeff had won four Grand National races and was fairly well-known by the time he entered the NASCAR Nextel Cup Series, he was in awe of the series and a little "gun-shy," he said. "I didn't know anything, much less how these cars drove. I had only run one race," he told the press.

Jeff and Ward were both first-year drivers in the NASCAR Nextel Cup Series in 1994. Jeff ran the full season for the Stavola brothers' team. Ward signed on with A.C. Dillard and was a regular test driver for Hoosier Tires at the time.

By March, Jeff had established himself as one of the year's toughest rookies. But he was anxious as he went into the Purolator 500 at Atlanta Motor Speedway in Georgia. It's the same speedway where, in 1992, his debut had ended in a crash after only three laps. This time rain had cancelled his test session.

Ward had won the Busch Grand National race at the track the year before. "This place had me scared to death," Jeff said. "I got a lot of help from Ward. He knows this track well."

By the race's midpoint, Jeff led the field by a half-lap. He led four times for 87 laps but eventually fell to fourth

Race fans fill the grandstand at the Atlanta Motor Speedway in Hampton, Georgia. Jeff's debut here in 1992 ended in a crash after only three laps.

position after he made a pit stop following the third yellow flag. (A solid yellow flag signals the racers to slow down when the track is dangerous because of a crash, debris, slick fluids, or rain.)

Pit stops have won or lost many a race for drivers. At some tracks, the cars only need 15 seconds to complete a lap. Each second a car is in the pit means it's behind that many seconds on the track. That's why it's important that the driver and team are in contact through two-way radios. The driver can explain problems, and the crew chief can give advice and direction to the driver as well as inform him on strategy. As the driver pulls into the pit lane, each crew member has been assigned a specific task, so multiple jobs are completed at one stop.

The problem is that the two-way radios are monitored by fans and other teams. Strategies may be overheard. Also, if a driver stops and the race is called off because of rain, he can lose his position on the track. With a lower finish, he gets fewer points.

Jeff Burton's pit crew works on his car during the 1997 Exide Batteries 400 at the Richmond International Raceway in Richmond, Virginia. Drivers and their teams communicate through two-way radios and keep pit stops as short as possible.

In September, disaster hit. Jeff was leading the Rookie of the Year race by 12 points over Joe Nemechek as the two prepared for the Miller 400 at the Richmond International Raceway in Virginia. Then Jeff was disqualified from the race when a NASCAR inspector discovered holes about the size of quarters in the tops of three roll bars. The bars are welded together to form a protective cage around the driver. Holes reduce the cage's ability to withstand impact, making the car less safe. They are drilled in the top of the safety cage to reduce weight, but they only save about one to two pounds and are a violation of NASCAR's safety regulations.

NASCAR kicked Jeff and the Stavola brothers' racing team out of the race and fined them $10,000, one of the biggest fines since Junior Johnson was kicked out of NASCAR in 1991.

Jeff, shaken and angry, said he wasn't aware of the holes. "You don't build anything when it comes to safety and then drill holes in it," he said. "I am one rookie who has made all the races . . . and to not make this race because of this is pretty hard to take."

By the end of his first full season in the Cup, Jeff had 30 starts, 2 top-5s, and 3 top-10s. He finished 24th in points. Above all else, in a year of talented rookies, he'd won the hotly contested battle for the 1994 Rookie of the Year title. During the season, he'd sometimes been chased by Joe Nemechek and Steve Grissom and sometimes came in after his brother Ward, Mike Wallace, John Andretti, and Loy Allen Jr.

"We battled all year long to win that rookie thing. I kept telling everybody it didn't matter, but it does," Jeff admitted, adding, "One thing the rookie thing has taught us is the importance of consistency."

The 1995 season opened with great promise for the young driver, but it quickly began to crumble. In April, for the first time that season, Jeff failed to qualify for a race—the Hanes 500 at the Martinsville Speedway. Since his owners were too far down in points standings, Jeff did not receive one of the provisional starting points. Those went instead to Michael Waltrip, Derrike Cope, Geoffrey Bodine, and John Andretti.

In October, Ward won his first Nextel Cup race. Ironically, up until this race, Jeff and Ward had had comparable careers, with both eventually winning in every series they'd competed in, but Jeff had always won in a series before Ward. This time, Ward had beaten Jeff to a first win, so Jeff felt even more pressure to collect his own victory.

Family comes first. Jeff celebates a victory with his daughter, Kimberle Paige, and his wife, Kim.

Jeff stayed with the Stavola brothers for two years, but by the middle of 1995, it was clear that the team was consistently unable to run out in front and had settled back to mid-pack.

"I can point to several races we ran in the top 12 and didn't finish because we broke motors or something dumb happened. But the way we performed, I was not displeased whatsoever," Jeff said.

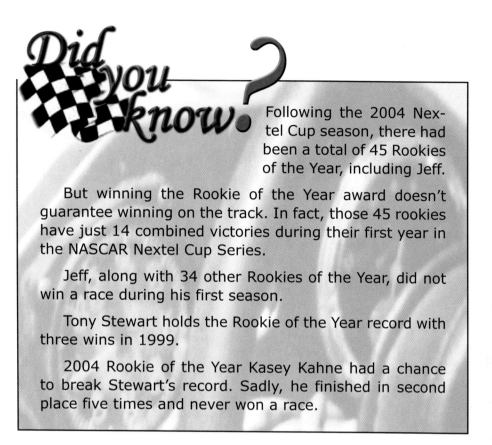

Did you know?

Following the 2004 Nextel Cup season, there had been a total of 45 Rookies of the Year, including Jeff.

But winning the Rookie of the Year award doesn't guarantee winning on the track. In fact, those 45 rookies have just 14 combined victories during their first year in the NASCAR Nextel Cup Series.

Jeff, along with 34 other Rookies of the Year, did not win a race during his first season.

Tony Stewart holds the Rookie of the Year record with three wins in 1999.

2004 Rookie of the Year Kasey Kahne had a chance to break Stewart's record. Sadly, he finished in second place five times and never won a race.

Also in 1995, Jeff and Kim's daughter, Kimberly Paige, was born, and Jeff let it be known that his family would always come first in his life.

When the 1995 season closed, Jeff was 32nd in points and had only 1 top-5 and 2 top-10s, a disappointing finish for the 1994 Rookie of the Year.

5

ROUSH SIGNS BURTON

Jack Roush, renowned owner of Roush Racing, had been watching Jeff for some time. Roush was looking for a driver for his new team. Jeff had discussed his interest in Roush's team with his longtime friend, Roush driver Mark Martin. Jeff felt he could work well with both Martin and Ted Musgrave, another Roush driver, but he had not considered himself to be in the running for the position.

Despite Jeff's ill-fated 1995 season, Roush made him an offer. Jeff liked the Stavola brothers, but going with Roush would give him a chance to reestablish himself. It could be a great career move.

In September 1995, Roush announced that Jeff would drive for his newly created third team. The team would be sponsored by Exide Batteries and be based in Charlotte, North Carolina, about an hour south of Roush's main base of operations in Liberty, North Carolina. Managing the operation would be legendary mechanic Buddy Parrott, who had won 18 races in two years with Rusty Wallace and had worked as crew chief for some of NASCAR's best drivers.

"We will rely more on Buddy to run a single car than we're currently relying on other people to run the others," Roush said.

Jack Roush, owner of Roush Racing, signed Jeff for his newly created third racing team in 1995. By 2005, nearly every Nextel Cup team had multicar teams.

Roush's two-car team of Martin and Musgrave would stay based in Liberty. This move gave Roush three separate Nextel Cup contenders, and each had its own crew.

Jeff had just entered the newest phenomenon in the Nextel Cup Series—multicar teams. At one time, such teams didn't exist, but by 2005, nearly every Nextel Cup team had at least two cars. Some, like Roush, had five cars. Because NASCAR only allows each car seven testing sessions per season, one of the advantages of multicar teams is that they can share important information from their different test drives. At the time, Roush's case meant that three teams got a total of 21 test drives to learn from.

Longtime friend and Roush teammate, Mark Martin (right) talks to Jeff before qualifying for the CarsDirect.com 400 at the Las Vegas Motor Speedway in March 2000.

Some wondered if the third team felt at odds by being in a different location, but Jeff soon quashed that rumor. "I don't feel like, and nobody on this team feels like we are slighted anything by being the brand-new team. The advantage is that we had some people who were willing to help us get started and give us some information," Jeff told *The Detroit News*.

However, the Exide team didn't find a home in Charlotte. Instead, they set up north of Charlotte in Dick Moroso's shops in Mooresville, North Carolina. Jeff also moved his family from South Boston to North Carolina, to be closer to the shop.

When Jeff first rolled out the No. 99 Exide Batteries Ford Thunderbird in Daytona, he came out as a strong contender for the Nextel Cup. (Ward was now driving a Pontiac for Bill Davis.)

By the time Jeff reached his hometown track in South Boston, Virginia, he had finished 5th at Daytona and 13th at Rockingham. He probably had the fastest car in South Boston and led three times for 53 laps, nearly winning. He was in the lead when the caution flag waved on lap 350, but he took a pit stop. He was fifth out of the pits and rapidly passed Rusty Wallace, but he couldn't pass teammate Ted Musgrave. The Roush team finished with Musgrave in third, Jeff fourth, Martin fifth. Martin later said he fought off an urge to race three-wide (side by side) with his teammates.

After three races, Jeff was second in points going into Atlanta for the Purolator 500.

"There's a heck of a lot less pressure being second than being 32nd," he said. "This might sound a bit pretentious, but I really expected to run this well. Racing is not complicated: it's putting the right people on the right team and letting them get to work."

But Jeff's hopes were dashed when, in the final minutes before the end of the morning practice, his car gave off a puff of steam and slowed. It had overheated. The crew cooled the engine and tried without success to patch the car together. Jeff's chance of qualifying for one of the 38 starting positions was low, and he wasn't eligible for a provisional spot because his team was new.

Team officials and Ford representatives jumped into action, asking Ford teams with provisional opportunities to stand on the qualifying time, giving Jeff an opportunity to beat their first-round qualifying time. Junie Donlavey, owner of the Fords driven by Mike Wallace, asked him to stand on his time. Wallace agreed.

Jeff ran his lap at 30.346 seconds, but he couldn't beat Wallace's 30.221 seconds for the 38th position. The missed start dropped Jeff to 14th in points.

With tears in his eyes, Jeff tried to explain to his team the pain of not qualifying for the race. Had it happened one week later, his new team would have been eligible for a spot. "Obviously, it's devastating," he said later.

By the next race, Jeff was literally back on the track. He placed 10th at the TranSouth Financial 400 in Darlington. And he just kept on going.

In August, Jeff was pleased but baffled after winning his first Nextel Cup pole at the Goodwrench 400 at Michigan International Speedway in Brooklyn, Michigan.

"Winning the pole means a lot because it's where we've really struggled; it's been our weak link. When we didn't make the field in Atlanta, I told them [the crew] we'd sit on the pole somewhere this year. And, this is the same car we didn't make it [with] in Atlanta."

Also, during open dates in the Cup schedule in June 1996, Jeff competed in the NASCAR Craftsman Truck Series events. So did NASCAR Nextel Cup Series champion Rusty Wallace. Both men were driving Ford pickups—Jeff for Roush Racing, Wallace for Penske South—and both were trying to qualify for the inaugural DeVilbiss SuperFinish 200 in late June at the Nazareth Speedway in Pennsylvania.

Both drivers made it to DeVilbiss, but neither won. Jeff started in 16th position and finished in 4th; Wallace started in 7th position and finished in 9th. At the end of the 1996 Craftsman Truck Series, Jeff ranked 42nd, with 4 starts, 1 top-5 and 3 top-10s.

Jeff returned to the Busch Series for his first race in that junior series since 1993. Like many of the Cup drivers, he was not actively seeking the Busch Series championship. He raced to gain publicity, to interest fans, and to learn the track before the next day's Cup race. In May, he competed at the

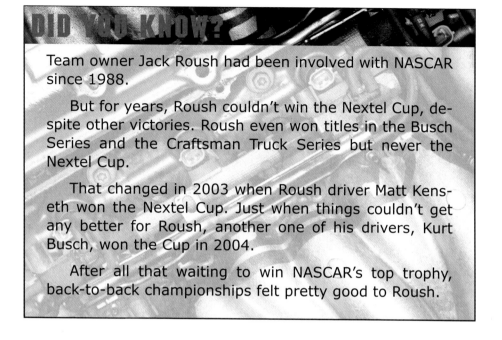

DID YOU KNOW?

Team owner Jack Roush had been involved with NASCAR since 1988.

But for years, Roush couldn't win the Nextel Cup, despite other victories. Roush even won titles in the Busch Series and the Craftsman Truck Series but never the Nextel Cup.

That changed in 2003 when Roush driver Matt Kenseth won the Nextel Cup. Just when things couldn't get any better for Roush, another one of his drivers, Kurt Busch, won the Cup in 2004.

After all that waiting to win NASCAR's top trophy, back-to-back championships felt pretty good to Roush.

Red Dog 300 at Lowe's Motor Speedway in Concord, North Carolina. He started in 7th position but finished 42nd in the field because of mechanical problems.

When the Nextel Cup Series season closed, Jeff was an impressive 13th in points, had 6 top-5s, 12 top-10s, and 1 pole, but he hadn't won a race. Would 1997 bring him a trip to Victory Lane?

6

WRECKS AND BREAKS

Jeff entered the 1997 Nextel Cup season as one of "the Underdogs," a select group of well-liked drivers who had been plagued with various problems in their quest for the Cup's championship. The esteemed group included John Andretti, Dave Marcis, Rick Mast, Kyle Petty, Darren Waltrip, and Michael Waltrip.

Impatient for a win, Jeff was anxious about the new season. But he needn't have worried; 1997 would prove to be Jeff's breakthrough year.

It started with the inaugural weekend of the Texas Motor Speedway outside Fort Worth, Texas. Rain fell heavily. Thursday's and Friday's qualifying rounds had been postponed, as had most of the practice sessions.

The track was besieged with problems. Water was oozing through holes onto the new track. Rain had caused potholes. There were concerns about the track's quad-oval design. Tempers were short. Spectators were muddy and wet but not complaining.

Without a qualifying time to establish the starting grid, NASCAR had lined up the cars according to its standard procedure. The top 35 places were determined by Winston Cup points, and the last 8 were given in order of the postmarks on entries for the event.

Jeff started out 1997 with a win at the Texas Motor Speedway after wrecks reduced the field to 27 cars.

It was a difficult track. Drivers were bewildered, owners frustrated, and both groups were uneasy. Their apprehension proved well-founded. By the end of the day, 8 of 10 yellow flags had flown because of wrecks, 21 cars were damaged or knocked out by accidents, and only 27 cars finished the 73 laps.

Jeff had an advantage. He'd been one of the few able to test drive before the rain, which meant he could tune his car's spring and shock selections to fit best with the Texas bowl.

Buddy Parrott was ready in the pits. In the ninth caution, 68 laps from the finish, Parrott called Jeff in for fuel.

"Some of the other leaders didn't come in until later in the caution. So that gave us track position. That's really what won the race for us," Jeff said.

After 96 starts in the Cup Series, Jeff had made it to Victory Lane.

Not everything went well that year. At the Michigan Speedway, Jeff Gordon lost control of his Chevrolet in turns three and four as he moved to the inside of Dale Earnhardt's Chevrolet. He spun in front of the Fords driven by Dick Trickle and Burton. Injured in the crash, which also took out primary cars for Gordon and Trickle for the Miller 400, Burton was taken to a hospital in Jackson, Michigan, and then released.

More than two weeks later, with bruises and muscle strains mostly healed, Jeff's leg still hurt. He had an MRI (magnetic resonance imaging) done on his leg. It was broken.

Would Jeff be able to drive in July at Daytona?

Parrott quipped, "You don't put on the brakes at Daytona so he should be fine." He went on to explain that Jeff's broken leg hadn't bothered him in driving. "His [bruised] ribs were the big thing because driving the race car is a seat of the pants thing, and if you're favoring your ribs you can't hold the steering wheel just right like you need to." He added that the doctors had provided Jeff a brace for his leg.

Jeff finished the Daytona 400 in eighth position, but this time Ward was hospitalized with a concussion after a nine-car crack-up that took place when the judges lifted the caution flag with only one lap to go. The track was littered with car parts and debris as cars jockeyed for the winning position.

Jeff took home his second career Cup victory at the New Hampshire International Speedway that same month. A gap of almost five seconds separated him from Dale Earnhardt's Chevrolet.

"I got a hell of a race team," Jeff said. "It's only a year and a half we've been together, and to get two wins and be as competitive as we are says a lot about this team."

Jeff talks to crew chief Frankie Stoddard (right) as he pushes his car along pit row during qualifying at the Martinsville Speedway in Martinsville, Virginia on September 25, 1998.

At an average speed of 117.194 mph, Jeff also broke Jeff Gordon's 1995 record of 107.029 mph.

By August, a rivalry was developing between Jeff and Gordon. At Darlington, Jeff's temper flared as he traded paint with Gordon in their charge for first- and second-place finishes.

Gordon recalled later that he saw Jeff coming and moved down because Jeff was making a run on him. "He plowed into the back of me and almost lifted the wheels off the ground.

My car kind of took off sideways. I don't think he was expecting that. It knocked him onto the apron," Gordon described.

Jeff had his side of the story. "I got under him and he cut me down," he told *Winston Cup Illustrated*. "I turned right on him because he turned left. I just didn't get him good enough. I thought [Dale] Jarrett was going to win the race, but I was going to do my best to make sure he [Gordon] didn't win the race because he cut down on me."

Burton added, "I would have got him, but I got the toe-in knocked out when we hit. . . . I tried to put him in the wall and I just missed him. . . . He [was] going for a million dollars. You can't blame him, but I'm going for a win, too, and I was going to do whatever I had to. I had him passed."

Gordon got his million. Jeff got second place.

In early September, Jeff had to hand the wheel over to relief driver Todd Bodine. An inner ear infection, which caused him to lose his balance and feel dizzy, sidelined him. Since he'd completed 68 laps in the New Hampshire, NASCAR rules allowed Jeff to gain points from Bodine's run. The No. 99 ended up 14th, and Jeff kept his 4th-place spot in the points race. The ear problem kept him from the qualifying rounds at Dover Downs, too. But he took a provisional spot and ended the race 11th.

By late September, Jeff was fully recovered. He charged to his third career Cup victory at Martinsville Speedway after NASCAR took the rare step of levying a stop-and-go penalty on leader Rusty Wallace.

Wallace had jumped ahead on consecutive restarts late in the race. The penalty dropped Wallace from 1st to 15th. Wallace claimed he never jumped the restart because he was the leader. NASCAR officials said the proper place for a restart is the gate at the exit of turn four, but Wallace accelerated about 100 feet from the crossover. A spokesman for NASCAR said the team had received two warnings about jumping the restart.

Jeff won, but only after Bobby Hamilton gave him a battle. Hamilton pushed the nose of his Pontiac ahead of Jeff's Ford. With Jeff on the outside groove, they battled side by side for about six laps. Finally, the No. 99 got in front of the pesky Pontiac. In the end, Jeff posted a 0.778-second victory over Dale Earnhardt, who had passed Hamilton with only five laps to go.

It was a day of success for the Burton family: Ward had taken the pole, and Jeff had won the race.

Jeff exploded into the top ranks of the Cup Series in 1997. He ended the year 4th in points, with 32 starts, 3 wins, 13 top-5s, and 18 top-10s. Also in the Busch Series, he had 13 starts, 2 wins, 9 top-5s, 10 top-10s, one pole, and was 26th in points.

Jeff had now won races in every type of series he had entered, but despite his successes, he didn't celebrate. He firmly believes doing so is inviting big trouble. He fears success might make him content and that contentment might ruin his edge on the track.

As the season drew to a close, Roush Racing moved from a three-car team to a five-car team and announced that Parrott, who'd overseen only Jeff's car in 1997, would be team manager for both Jeff's and Martin's cars. Martin's team would be housed in the same shop. Jimmy Fennig would continue as Martin's crew chief, but Jeff would enter the 1998 season with a new crew chief, Frankie Stoddard.

In 1998, one journalist wrote, "If Jeff Gordon had never been born, we'd all be talking about Jeff Burton right now." Jeff was that good, but to win the championship, his new

Jeff Gordon (No. 24) and Jeff Burton (No. 99) in action September 12, 1998 during the NASCAR Exide 400 at the Richmond International Raceway in Richmond, Virginia. The two Jeffs began quite a rivalry during the 1997 season.

team would need to meld together fast. He was again poised to be a championship contender and debuted the new No. 99—a Ford Taurus.

The year didn't start well. The crew suffered engine problems that put them out of two races. On two occasions, wrecks cut their days short. Problems in the pits and in pole qualifying plagued the team all year.

The Exide team's pit stops improved dramatically over the course of the year, as did the adjustments they made to the car. Jeff and Stoddard were quickly becoming a powerful team.

At the New Hampshire International Speedway in July, Jeff made his first trip of the season to Victory Lane. Of the final 221 laps, Jeff had led all but 30.

Jeff was sure he was the car to beat after his final pit stop. "You know four laps into a run if you've got what it takes or not. . . . I said, 'Man, we've got it made. Don't wreck, don't miss a shift, don't do something stupid, and we'll win this race.'"

"Nobody could touch [Burton]," said Jeff Gordon, who came in third. "He definitely was in a different league than the rest of us."

It's Jeff's favorite track on the circuit. "I prefer this track over the rest because I have competed in every [Nextel] Cup race there and have won in two divisions, [Nextel] Cup and Busch Grand National," he explained.

The team kept going strong, finishing in the top-10 in five out of the next seven races. By the fall race at Richmond International Raceway, they had pooled their talents and become a winning team.

Jeff dominated the field during most of the race at Richmond. He led six times for a total of 203 laps, but with 10 laps to go, rival Gordon caught up with him. In a side-by-side battle, they ran down the stretch toward the checkered flag. Jeff was in the high groove and Gordon in the low groove. It was the last caution of the race that decided Jeff's destiny.

"We caught that caution just right and had an awesome stop. We were in trouble on the long runs," Jeff said. The caution set up the short run to the finish. Gordon came in second.

Despite some problems, Jeff finished the year with a Nextel Cup career high of $2,626,987 in winnings. He had 33 starts, 18 top-5s, and 23 top-10s—more than all but two drivers. Jeff won twice but finished fifth in the final standings—one point short of his fourth position in 1997. Still, it had been a remarkable year. In the Busch Series, he had

Though Jeff Burton and Jeff Gordon were rivals at one time, Gordon ended up in a class all by himself.

That's nothing against Jeff Burton. But Gordon's four Nextel Cup titles and three Daytona 500 wins set him apart from almost every driver in NASCAR history.

Richard Petty and Dale Earnhardt Sr. are tied for the most Nextel Cup championships with seven. Gordon's four series titles are the second-best overall.

As of early 2005, Gordon had 70 race wins. He was seventh on the all-time wins list. Jeff Burton had 17 total wins and was tied for 37th place.

Gordon might not get seven championships, but his place in history is certainly secure.

13 starts, 3 victories, 7 top-5 finishes, 9 top-10s, 2 poles, and finished 30th in points.

Jeff drove into 1999 as a man growing accustomed to winning.

A ROLLER-COASTER CAREER

Ⅰn 1999, the racer to beat was Jeff Gordon. He was after his third Nextel Cup championship in a row and his fourth overall. To compete against Gordon, Jeff would have to improve his qualifying, be consistent, and finish more races than he had in 1998. As the season began, he felt ready.

"At some point in your career, you have to get over that potential label and start doing it," Jeff said.

And like all the Nextel Cup contenders at the season opening at Daytona, Jeff hoped 1999 would be his year to be the Nextel Cup Series champion. Many thought he'd make it, too. He was calmer, took losses better, and had learned to work well within the Roush organization and with his crew. And his working partnership with Mark Martin was expanding onto the track.

"It's a strain, obviously, when you have two competitive teams. So, we just work extra hard to make sure everybody knows that we have the same opportunities," Jeff told *USA Today*. Martin commented, "[Burton] has the personality that makes the deal work."

Jeff left Daytona with a disappointing DNF [did not finish] after a 12-car chain-reaction crash between turns three

A 12-car chain reaction crash forced Jeff out of the Daytona 500 on February 14, 1999.

and four on lap 135. Dale Jarrett's No. 88 had been tapped by another car and spun sideways. It went down onto the apron, and came back across the track, then was hit and turned upside down. The crash took out the cars of Jeff Burton, Mark Martin, Joe Nemechek, Geoffrey Bodine, and Elliott Sander, among others.

As expected, Gordon won the race and the pole.

But at the Las Vegas Motor Speedway, Jeff Burton made it to Victory Lane, and Ward was right by his side. For four laps around the 1.5-mile track, the brothers dueled for the lead, racing side by side as Jeff tried to overtake Ward's Pontiac. As he was going into the second turn on the 257th lap of the 267-lap event, Jeff slipped around the outside of Ward's car. He then began pulling away and won the race by 1.074 seconds.

"I tried to crowd Jeff as much as I could in the exit corner, but I couldn't wreck my brother," Ward recalled.

Jeff admitted, "I kind of giggled in the race car because [Nextel] Cup racing is a really big deal, and for two brothers to be racing for a win in one of the biggest races of the year, that's pretty special."

At the Atlanta Motor Speedway in Georgia, Gordon won and Jeff dropped to fourth position, only to shoot back to win the rain-shortened race at Darlington, which was called after lap 164 of the 293-lap event. Gordon had won the pole, but he came in third.

Neither Gordon nor Jeff would win the next four races, but at the California Speedway, Gordon came in first, Jeff second. The war of the Jeffs was heating up, and NASCAR fans loved it.

"My way of racing is that you just run as hard as you can all the time," Jeff told *The Charlotte Observer.* "What [Gordon] does such a good job of is playing 'possum;' you don't ever know if he can't run or if he's not running. He might be able to run faster than you, but he doesn't let you know until it's too late for you to do anything about it."

Gordon took the pole at Richmond in the spring, but he came in 31st to Jeff's 37th place finish. In the Nextel Cup at Lowe's Motor Speedway, Gordon came in third, and Jeff wrecked.

At the same speedway a week later, Bobby Labonte was the one to beat, and he took the pole.

Then there was the $1 million bonus that Labonte, Jeff, Ward, Gordon, and Mike Skinner had all earned a chance to win in the No Bull 5. But to get it, they had to win the race. On that May weekend, the race was close and would be won in the final pit stops.

Interestingly, Labonte and Jeff were facing the same problems in the corners as they went into the final 30 laps. The question to each crew was whether to tighten or loosen the car. If a car is "tight," the front of the car wants to go to the outside wall and not turn into the corner. If a car is "loose," the rear of the car wants to slide out and go toward the outside wall.

Labonte's crew added an extra pound of air pressure in his tires to help loosen his car for the final 30 laps. Stoddard chose to make a lot of adjustments to Jeff's No. 99 and to tighten the stock car. Stoddard had felt it was too loose to run with Labonte's, so the crew adjusted the car for a 30-lap run, not a 70-lap run. It was a risky move. Afraid the plan might be overheard and tip their hand, Stoddard and Jeff didn't use radio communications.

"I wasn't sure we had made the right moves," Stoddard admitted later.

On the final pit stop, Jeff's time was 17.3 seconds; Labonte's 17.4. Out of the pits, Jeff took the lead, but Labonte took it over on lap 381. Jeff pushed the No. 99's throttle harder, and three laps later he was in the lead. Labonte closed the gap to 0.574 seconds, but he couldn't overtake Jeff. Gordon had trouble with handling and finished 39th.

It was Jeff's third win of the season and eighth career victory in the Cup Series. He had won the $1 million bonus and was ahead in points.

Gordon took the pole in June at the Michigan Speedway, but Jarrett won. Gordon came in second, Jeff third, and Ward fourth.

At the Pocono 500, Labonte won, and Gordon was second. Jeff crossed the finish line in 36th place with the cars after him all out because of accidents or engine problems.

Jeff celebrates his victory in the Jiffy Lube 300 at the New Hampshire International Speedway in Loudon, New Hampshire. He clocked the quickest pit stop of the day at three seconds.

Gordon took the pole and race at Infineon Raceway in Sonoma, California, one of only two road racing venues in Nextel Cup. Jeff finished 24th after his gearbox broke entering turn 11. And at the Daytona 400, Jeff came in 3rd, Gordon 21st.

Jeff moved into the lead at the NHIS 300 after rookie Tony Stewart ran out of fuel two laps before he would likely have taken his first Cup victory.

With 10 laps to go, Stoddard pitted Jeff for the quickest pit stop of the day—three seconds. Jeff, who had started in 38th position, won the race. Stoddard's fuel strategy had worked. The rival Jeffs were neck and neck with four victories each.

Gordon had taken the pole and placed third in the race. After having led the race for 103 laps, rookie Tony Stewart finished 10th and stormed out of the track. He later apologized.

Jeff Gordon came back to win the pole at the Indianapolis Motor Speedway, in Indiana, and then came in third, with Jeff Burton in fifth and Ward in sixth. Gordon went on to win at the fall Watkins Glen International, in New York, where Jeff came in 13th.

Ward took the pole at the Michigan Speedway 400, but Labonte won the race. Gordon came in 2nd, and Jeff was in 37th—after a wreck in which Tony Stewart passed and clipped the No. 99, sending it to the wall. At the Bristol Motor Speedway in Tennessee, Gordon was 4th and Jeff was 17th.

The odds of winning two Cup races at the same track in the same year are poor. They are worse if both races are shortened by rain. But Jeff Burton did just that with his win at the Southern 500 at Darlington, the oldest superspeedway event.

"Deciding whether to pit or not to pit for tires [after the second red flag] was really, really stressful," he said. "I figured there was no way it could [end in the rain] twice in one year."

Ward was second behind his brother. Gordon finished 13th. Jeff collected a second $1 million bonus, as did a lucky fan who had picked Jeff as the winner. Jeff and Gordon were now tied, each with five wins. But neither won a Nextel Cup event for several races afterward.

By the September race at NHIS, the racers and crews were tired. It was the seventh race of 12 straight race weekends. Rain caused the cancellation of the practice and pole qualifying.

"This is a grueling schedule," Jeff told the *Boston Herald*. "It's a physically and mentally hard time of the year because we run so many races in a row. You can utilize this day to get everybody a little rest and to spend a little time talking about something other than rear ends and transmissions and springs and shocks."

Then Gordon broke through. He won the Martinsville 500, with Jeff placing 9th, and the following week's Lowe's Motor Speedway 500, where Jeff placed 37th. That would be Gordon's last trip to Victory Lane for the season.

Jeff, though, would win one more race in 1999, the Rock's 400. For the third time during the 1999 season, Ward came in second.

At the end of the Nextel Cup season, Gordon had won seven races to Jeff's six. In the Cup standings, for the second year, Jeff came in fifth, with 4,733 points; Gordon finished sixth with 4,620 points. Jeff had three DNFs and six finishes outside of the top 30. His inconsistency had kept him on a roller coaster and cost him the Cup.

In the Busch standings Jeff started 14 times—fewer than half the starts of the winner—and had 1 win, 7 top 5s, and 12 top 10s. He ended the season with 2,091 points.

"It was an up-and-down year for us," Jeff told *NASCAR Online*. "We're proud of our six wins but we're disappointed at the number of races we didn't finish. To be a champion, you have to be competitive in every race. We had some mechanical failures, and I made some mistakes. If you want to be competitive, you can't do that."

In 2000, the No. 99 debuted with a new paint scheme and graphics. While the original colors of black, silver, and pink were still used, the hood was white, lightning bolt graphics decorated the doors, and royal blue was added to the front portion of the car.

The car may have looked different, but the 2000 season began with familiar success. At the Daytona 500, on February 20, Jeff finished in second place behind Dale Jarrett. For the season, he finished a career-best third in the points standings and won four races.

That year ended up being Jeff's best season ever.

Many NASCAR Nextel Cup drivers would be thrilled to finish in the top 15 every year, especially if it gave them a shot at the new "Chase for the Nextel Cup" playoff system.

But with the high expectations for Jeff, not being a championship contender was disappointing. After his stellar 2000 season, Jeff never found the same success again with Roush Racing.

He finished 10th in 2001 and 12th in each of the two years after that.

Ward wasn't having much success either. During Jeff's great 2000 season, Ward finished 10th. He dropped to 14th in 2001, then crashed into 21st and 25th in the following two seasons.

After a 32nd place finish in the 2004 season standings, Ward was released from his No. 0 car. When the 2005 season began, he was still looking for a new job.

Jeff, meanwhile, got the last of his 17 career wins on Oct. 28, 2001 in the Checker Auto Parts/Dura-Lube 400 at

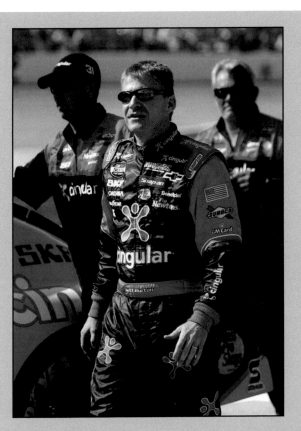

Jeff prior to qualifying for the Samsung/RadioShack 500 race at Texas Motor Speedway on April 15, 2005.

Phoenix International Raceway. He led 102 laps that day en route to the victory.

Since that time, Jeff hasn't been back to Victory Lane. Entering the 2005 season, Jeff had a 112-race winless streak, one of the longest in Nextel Cup racing.

In August 2004, Jeff decided to part ways with his long-time car owner, Jack Roush. A new opportunity beckoned at Richard Childress Racing. Most important, it was a fresh start with a stable car.

DID YOU KNOW?

Richard Childress became Jeff's car owner in the summer of 2004.

Childress is a former NASCAR driver, but he will be forever remembered for one thing: owning Dale Earnhardt Sr.'s No. 3 car.

Earnhardt Sr. was killed in 2001 during the last lap of the Daytona 500. Many regard "The Intimidator" as the best driver in history.

Childress owned Earnhardt Sr.'s car during six Nextel Cup championship seasons. Childress has won titles in the Busch Series and Craftsman Truck Series during his 35 years in NASCAR.

It's safe to say Jeff is driving for an owner with plenty of winning experience.

There was reason to be optimistic. To Jeff, age equals experience, and he said he's in the best shape of his life heading into 2005.

"I'm a whole lot smarter, without a doubt," he said. "I know how to handle things better, mentally I'm just so much stronger than I was. Physically, I can do things today I couldn't do five years ago. I know that sounds stupid, but I'm in better shape today than I was in high school. "I wouldn't go back and be 25 for anything."[8]

Will Jeff win a Nextel Cup championship before his career ends? As he said during his prime years, "What kind of a driver and team player would I be if I didn't think we had a good chance to win the championship going into every season?"

NOTES

Chapter 1

1. NASCAR media teleconference transcript; November 9, 2004

2. Ibid.

3. *The Associated Press*; March 2, 2003.

4. Ibid.

5. *USA Today*; January 20, 2005; Page 11C.

6. Personal interview notes.

7. Ibid.

Chapter 7

8. Personal interview notes.

CHRONOLOGY

1967 Born on June 29, in South Boston, Virginia.

1974 Begins racing go-karts at the local track, South Boston Speedway.

1984 Has his first stock car victory at South Boston Speedway.

1986 Becomes the youngest driver in NASCAR history to win a late-model stock car race.

1987 Is track co-champion at Orange County Speedway, in Virginia.

1988 Voted most popular driver at South Boston Speedway.

1989 Runs first full season in the NASCAR Busch Grand National Series.

1990 Wins his first Busch race at Martinsville Speedway; continues to get one win a year in the Busch Series, in South Boston, 1991.

1993 Enters his first Nextel Cup Series race at the New Hampshire International Speedway, qualifying for sixth position; joins the Stavola brothers' team.

1994 Receives NASCAR Nextel Cup's Rookie of the Year award.

1995 Signs on late in the year with Roush Racing.

1996 Wins his first Nextel Cup pole at Michigan International Speedway and finishes the season 13th in points—a career high; races in the Busch and Nextel Cup Series.

1997 Has his first career win in the Nextel Cup Series at the Texas Motor Speedway; wins two more events in the Nextel Cup and finishes the season with a career-high fourth in points.

1998 Finishes the year with a career high in winnings and fifth in the final standings with two wins, 18 top-5s, 23 top-10s—more than all but two other drivers.

1999 Finishes fifth in the standings; extends his contract with Roush Racing through 2005.

2000 Takes second at the Daytona 500; wins the CarsDirect.com 400 at the Las Vegas Motor Speedway. Finishes with a career-best third in points.

2001 Slips to 10th in points. Wins two races, including the final one of his career to date.

2002 Finishes 12th in points and did not win a race for the first time since 1996.

2003 Places again 12th in points, having just three top 5 finishes.

2004 Leaves Roush Racing; signs with Richard Childress.

2005 Finishes 29th at the Daytona 500.

STATISTICS

NASCAR Nextel Cup Series

Year	Races	Wins	Top 5	Top 10	Poles	Point Earnings	Standings
1993	1	0	0	0	0	$9, 550	
1994	30	0	2	3	0	$594, 700	24th
1995	29	0	1	2	0	$630, 770	32nd
1996	30	0	6	12	1	$884, 303	13th
1997	32	3	13	18	0	$2, 296, 614	4th
1998	33	2	18	23	0	$2, 626, 987	5th
1999	34	6	18	23	0	$5, 725, 399	5th
2000	34	4	15	22	1	$5, 121, 350	3rd
2001	36	2	8	16	0	$3, 866, 330	10th
2002	36	0	5	14	0	$3, 863, 220	12th
2003	36	0	3	11	0	$3, 846, 880	12th
2004	36	0	2	6	0	$3, 695, 070	18th
2005	1*	0	0	0	0	$256, 420	28th
Career	368	17	91	150	2	$35, 360, 965	

*as of February 24, 2005

FURTHER READING

Buckley, James. *NASCAR: Speedway Superstars*. Reader's
    Digest Children's Publishing, 2004.

Canfield, Jack, et al. *Chicken Soup for the NASCAR Soul*.
    HCI, 2003.

Doeden, Matt. *NASCAR's Wildest Wrecks*. Edge Books,
    2005.

Fresina, Michael J., ed. *Thunder and Glory: The 25 Most
    Memorable Races in NASCAR Winston Cup History*.
    Triumph Books, 2004.

Garrow, Mark. *Dale Earnhardt: The Pass in the Grass
    and Other Incredible Moments from Racing's Greatest
    Legend*. Sports Publishing, 2001.

Hembree, Mike. *Dale Earnhardt Jr.: Out of the Shadow of
    Greatness*. Sports Publishing, 2003.

McLaurin, Jim. *NASCAR's Most Wanted: The Top 10
    Book of Outrageous Drivers, Wild Wrecks, and Other
    Oddities*. Potomac Books, 2001.

Richard, Jon. *Fantastic Cutaway: Speed*. Copper
    Beech, 1997.

Stewart, *Mark. Auto Racing: A History of Cars and Fearless
    Drivers*. Franklin Watts, 1999.

Woods, Bob. *NASCAR: The Greatest Races*. Reader's
    Digest, 2004.

BIBLIOGRAPHY

"Burton aims to become talk to teams again." *Associated Press*, March 2, 2003.

Burton, Jeff. Interview by NASCAR media teleconference, November 9, 2004.

Burton, Jeff. Interview by Jeff Gluck, January 20, 2004.

Duke Children's Hospital & health Center. *http://duke health1.org/childrens_services/press_release_gain.asp.*

Jenkins, Chris. "Burton sees team taking turn for better." *USA Today*, January 20, 2005, 11C.

ADDRESSES

Jeff Burton Fan Club
6000 Fairview Road
Suite 635
Charlotte, NC 28210

NASCAR
P.O. Box 2875
Daytona Beach, FL 32120
(386) 253-0611

INTERNET SITES

www.jeffburton.com

> *The interactive Jeff Burton Fan Club website features Jeff Burton's latest news. It has video interviews with Jeff and videos of Jeff using the different kinds of equipment in his car to prepare for a race—including his safety strap, ignition switch, gloves, and even sunglasses. One page teaches you about the different parts of the car.*

www.rcrracing.com

> *Richard Childress Racing Network's official website is full of information about all of the RCR teams. It features pictures of all the team's cars and links to each driver's website. It also features a virtual tour the Richard Childress Racing Museum.*

www.nascar.com

> *This website is the best place to start learning more about NASCAR. It has the latest results and driver standings, with pages where readers can learn more about the sport in general.*

www.jayski.com

For readers interested in more in-depth NASCAR news, Jayski's Silly Season site is the site to visit. Every day, Jayski collects facts and rumors from all over the country and puts it on the website. Many news items that happen in NASCAR appear somewhere on Jayski.com first.

Photo Credits:

Stephen Lynch www.lynch2.com: Cover, 7; AP/Wide World Photos: 8, 9, 16, 18, 23, 26, 30, 35, 37, 44, 47, 51; © Stephanie Maze/CORBIS: 12, 13; © Reuters/CORBIS: 29; © Getty Images: 24, 40.

INDEX

ABOUT THE AUTHORS

June Ford is a nationally published writer and ghostwriter. She is a former journalist and a newspaper and magazine editor. Ford has written, edited, proofread, and coordinated projects for national and regional publishing houses and magazines. Since 1987, she has owned and operated her own company, JFE Editorial Services. She is a writer-in-residences for the state of Texas. Ford has a bachelor's degree from Texas Christian University in Fort Worth, Texas.

Jeff Gluck covers NASCAR, high schools, and the Atlantic Coast Conference for the *Rocky Mount Telegram*, in North Carolina. A University of Delaware graduate, Gluck has also lived in California, Minnesota, and Colorado, visiting a total of 45 states along the way. Gluck has covered the Super Bowl, the Daytona 500, the ACC basketball tournament, and has attended three NCAA Final Fours.

Gluck and his wife, Jaime, reside in Rocky Mount, North Carolina.